TEN LITTLE STUDI

1

GORDON JACOB

Andante con moto

6

9

Andantino

10

Allegro vivace

TEN LITTLE STUDIES

1

GORDON JACOB

Andante cantabile

2

Alla marcia viva

Printed in Great Britain

OXFORD UNIVERSITY PRESS, MUSIC DEPARTMENT, GREAT CLARENDON STREET, OXFORD OX2 6DP

6

Tempo di Valse lento

poco rit...

7

Alla Sarabanda

8

Allegro scherzando

8

Allegro scherzando